Healing

ANHTUẤN ĐỖ

Quill Hawk Publishing

Cover Designed by Ava Wood with Fins and Feathers Designs

ISBN: 978-1-965142-09-7 (Paperback)

ISBN: 978-1-965142-10-3 (eBook)

LCCN: 2024919313

Contents

*I hope you're kinder to
yourself today.*

Tell Anhtuan about this book's journey.

Profile Name:

_____

Book Number:

_____

Introduction

As the title says, this is my story of healing. It's a compilation of thoughts, journal entries, notes from my therapy sessions, and conversations from January to May of 2023. I'll share some of the things that happened in my life; I'll share some of the tools that helped me; and most importantly, I'll share the voice in my head.

It's the voice that I heard the most. In my case, it was the harshest, meanest, and most unforgiving voice. I suspect for many of you, it's the same.

In those five months, I understood that it's also the only voice I can change.

This is how I changed mine.

At the start of the year, that voice told me that I wasn't worthy of this world; that I wasn't capable of doing any good, and that it was time to find a way out.

Now, I know I belong.

I hope that by sharing my story, someone with a similar voice will seek to change theirs. Then, I'll have made that person's day a bit better... a bit more bearable.

That's all I want. I want to make sure you understand that you belong in this world no matter what you do.

We all have our own journey.

This is mine.

Overview

My name is Anhtuan Do, and over the first two weeks of March 2023, I wrote a full screenplay about my parents. During the Vietnam War, my dad received a scholarship to come to the United States and study economics at Vanderbilt University. In 1973, during the height of the war, he traveled alone to Nashville while my mom and three-year-old sister stayed in Vietnam.

Right before his graduation in May of 1975, South Vietnam lost the war. My mom and sister got stuck. My parents completely lost touch and couldn't speak to each other for three years. They didn't really know what happened to the other.

In 1978, my mom and sister snuck out on fishing boats, reuniting everyone at 6:00 PM on Friday, June 16th of that year.

But that's their story. I want to tell you mine.

I went to the University of Notre Dame in South Bend, IN, and started my career in consulting. I went on to help grow a company into the Fortune 500, an annual list curated by *Fortune* magazine of the largest 500 companies based on revenue. Now, I run IT for an incredible start-up—wildly successful by most people's measure.

My story begins in April of 2022. I got an assignment to go to the Middle East. I had no idea what to expect, so I decided that I needed to get a life insurance policy. It was well overdue, and if anything happened to me, my family needed to be taken care of.

Luckily, my dad sold life insurance. I called him and we started going through the seemingly millions of different options. Six months later, we settled on the parameters. My family already had a vacation planned in the UK, so I told my dad I'd sign when we got back.

I remember the exact moment the contract was sent to my inbox. It was early December. The sun was shining through the window, adding glare to my monitor. I opened the file and found the two most important pieces of information: the payout amount and the beneficiary. Both were right. I digitally signed. I clicked submit.

Within seconds, I got the fully executed document. My first thought was, "How do I make it look like an accident?"

Over the next couple of days, I called my dad and probed him a bit. He said, "You can't die in the first two years. You do, and they'll investigate, and with anything fishy, they won't pay because of the amount you bought."

To pump myself up, I told myself, "I can do two more years, I've done 42 already. It will go away. It's gone away every other time I've thought about it since I was 12."

This time it didn't.

Every single day, all I could do was think of different ways to make sure it looked like an accident. I had it all laid out.

Then the middle of January came, and my wife and I separated.

My 42-foot brick wall holding out a tidal wave of unprocessed pain fell to pieces. The water pummeled into me. I had two options: sink or swim.

I wanted to sink. I wanted to sink so badly. But my kids kept me here. They needed me. So I swam—or really, I treaded.

I called my mom the next morning. She picked up and put me on speaker with my dad. Before I said a word, I started to cry.

"Stop crying and be a man," my mom said. That was all she knew. It's how she was raised.

After a few dazed minutes of listening, I said, "Goodbye."

Stunned, I hung up the phone. I stared at it for what felt like an eternity.

Then something finally clicked. It wasn't that something was wrong with me. Something was wrong with the way I grew up.

There was a reason I didn't love myself.

The next morning, I called my sister and replayed the scene almost exactly the same way. She let me speak. And she let me cry. And when I was done, she said, "It's okay, I'll help you through it."

At that moment, I realized that I had a third option. It wasn't just sink or swim.

There was a different way to live life.

My sister was there to help me. I told my boss that I needed an hour a day, and without any question, he said yes. I didn't tell him why, and I wasn't asking for permission.

He gave it anyway.

That's when my healing began. I started with the thought that I needed to get therapy nearby, that having in-person sessions would be best. But I couldn't find a therapist that felt right. Very soon after, my brother-in-law recommended a mental health professional based in the Midwest for men going through divorce.

He had some conditions. "You've got to do the work, you need to join my support group, and you MUST be engaged ... well, if you want it to work," he said.

I didn't care what conditions he had.

I. Dug. In.

I came as close to committing myself to an institution as you can without moving in.

Every waking hour when I wasn't on the job or with the kids, I dealt with my past. The support group was a free-flowing stream of human connection. The first time I spoke with a support group guy, I was so flustered. I couldn't speak clear sentences. Sometimes I would just cry.

It didn't matter where I was: the library, the car, at work. Every conversation started with my tears. And without fail, every single response was, "It's okay. I understand. I've been there."

For the first time in my 42 years of life, I didn't feel alone.

Over the next ten weeks, I conservatively did about 400 hours of therapy. Assuming that traditional therapy is an hour a week, I did the equivalent of eight years. As the weeks passed, I started to notice the world around me. A tree swaying in the wind seemed peaceful. The birds flying by were majestic. Fog felt like a cloud gingerly touching the ground.

My inner pain transformed. The tidal wave became a flowing stream. That stream brought grass, bees, birds, trees, and eventually a small park bench where I could sit with my guitar and journal.

On March 1, my therapy shifted from forgiveness to belonging. The next day, the first scene of *Reunion* came to me. At 11:58 p.m. on March 16, I finished the first draft of *Reunion*, my parents' story.

After writing their story, I realized I needed to tell mine. Because if I told mine, one day, one person would hear it and seek help. It will have saved a life.

It didn't matter if 99 out of 100 people were uncomfortable with it. They could choose to leave and not listen. But one person... that one person who needed to hear it would hopefully seek help.

So I started with my team at work, and then my family. Now I speak freely about it. When I told my boss—the same boss who gave me an hour a day without question—he asked, "How do you know it won't come back?"

I didn't immediately have an answer. I just knew. I'd committed to the work for the rest of my life. Somehow, that answer didn't seem adequate to me.

Eventually, the answer came in possibly the most mundane task of the day.

It's my job to take the dogs out every morning. I used to hate it. The alarm would go off, or a dog would bark, and I would immediately feel dread. My aggravation would fester, and I'd get annoyed at how long it took them to do their business.

Today ... today, I put their leashes on. I put on my coat, and when I step outside, I immediately look up at the sky. I stand there in awe.

Whether it's sunny, cold, or rainy, something beautiful catches my eye.

I think to myself, "This beautiful sky connects every single person in the world ... including me."

And it makes me feel like I belong.

So I'll tell my story. And when I'm done, if you want me to listen to yours, I'll listen.

I'll listen. I'll cry with you, and when you're done telling me your story, I'll say, "It's okay. I understand. I've been there." Then I'll add, "And just like me, I know *you* belong."

A New Start

January 30, 2023

Why did I start this journey? That's a good question. It started now because this is when it was supposed to start. One week and four days ago, my world collapsed.

But in the collapse, The Universe sent help. It connected me to a mental health professional. He connected me to a support group.

Why start journaling now? I don't know, one of the guys in the support group suggested that I start journaling. So one week and four days later, here I am documenting my journey.

Who knows why?

Programs

January 19, 2023

Therapy Notes:

I have been programmed. That programming comes from my childhood. It's a strong program. In my case, it's version 42. I need to reprogram myself.

That takes time.

Some of my programs:

- I need constant physical contact and reassurance. v42.

- I feel abandoned and jealous when not involved. v42.

- I feel guilty whenever someone isn't happy. v42.

What do I want my programs to be?

- I am comfortable in my own skin. vFinal.

- I am comfortable and confident in my relationships. vFinal.

- I am only responsible for my own happiness. *vFinal*.

Logic

January 21, 2023

I do not start this day believing I am a good person. I don't end this day believing it either, but there's a seed.

Will it grow? I don't know, but it's the first time I'm questioning it.

My mental health professional uses logic to get me to acknowledge its possibility.

Therapy Notes:

Reason 1

- Go back to when I was a baby. Is that baby a good person?

- Yes, that baby is a good person.

- I am the same person as that baby.

Reason 2

- What about today? When I wake up, do I immediately wish harm on anyone?

- No?

- I'm a good person.

Thoughts:

- That's my therapist's opinion. He has to say that.

- Is it technically possible? I guess.

- Really though, it's for other people, not me.

Negative Feelings

January 21, 2023

Therapy Notes:

- Everybody has negative feelings. The problems begin when I let those negative feelings run my life.

- I don't think negative thoughts "on purpose."

- I can't think of two opposite things at the same moment in time.

- I can't think, "You're not worthy"

and "You're amazing" in the same literal second.

Thoughts:

My brain is starting to think some of this makes sense. I know my brain can't technically "multi-task." Even if I shift from one task to another incredibly fast, I can only focus on one thing at a time.

I think ...

More Logic

January 21, 2023

Therapy Notes:

- Events have no meaning except the ones I give them.

- My most precious real estate is not outside, it's *inside*.

- I believe my feelings are true, no matter what anybody says.

Thoughts:

- Maybe too much too fast? I don't know. This is harder for me to grasp.

- I still write it down.

Science

January 21, 2023

Therapy Notes:

The amygdala controls the chemicals in the body. It sends information to the prefrontal cortex for logical reasoning, but also sends a tiny bit of information to the pituitary gland to release chemicals enabling the fight or flight response.

You can't control the latter part. Any situation resembling trauma from your childhood induces a release of chemicals in your body akin to the ones from childhood.

Thoughts:

In my case, not ever receiving hugs as a child caused me to feel unworthy. So today, when I don't get a hug, I feel unworthy. Same chemicals.

Conclusion, I can't just choose to feel okay. Yet.

Attitude is not the source. It's the symptom. I need to go and resolve the original issue first.

1st Support Group Member

January 23, 2023

These guys are literally dispersed around the world. Nobody is close enough for me to meet in person, so it's group chats and phone calls.

I've only seen this guy's name in the chat. He sees my introduction post in the group and suggests that we speak.

I run IT for a start-up, and he is in tech. Today, I work from the Princeton Public Library.

I can't go into the office. I feel like I need to be in a place where no one knows me. I'm in the lobby so that I can actually talk.

He asks me to tell him my story.

I can't stop the tears.

Embarrassed, I walk outside into the cold New Jersey January. I don't want to make the other people in the lobby uncomfortable.

He says, "It's okay. I understand. I've been there."

I found the right group.

Golden Books

January 25, 2023

What are Golden Books? Golden Books are a way to relive your childhood memories. They're an account of the past that has caused you pain. They can be specific incidents, or groups of incidents that stay with you.

My mental health professional has me draw out Little Golden Books for each one.[1] "Create simple titles, titles that little-you would identify with," he guides.

I use them as a starting point for what I need to "clear." "Nobody has a perfect 'Family of Origin,' so you should be able to come up with 10-15 Golden Books by next week," he said.

I started coming up with them during the session. By the end of the hour, I had 14 Golden Books.

Before going to sleep, I had 33.

Ho'oponopono

I share with the guys that I'm struggling with all of the outside distractions and inside voices. Everything is so loud.

ALL OF THE DAMN TIME. THEY'RE ALL SO LOUD.

"Have you heard of the Ho'oponopono? Look it up," someone responds.[1]

I open Google. Turns out it's an ancient Hawaiian practice of forgiveness. It translates to "cause things to move back in balance."[2] It's four simple phrases. Four lines that I can repeat so easily. So quickly.

I'm sorry.

Please forgive me.

Thank you.

I love you.[3]

I start to do it everywhere I go. I say it to myself when the voices come out. I say it when I'm down. I say it when I feel other people's pain. The key is that I'm saying it to myself.

Every time I focus on it, I feel a bit of relief.

It's exactly what I'm looking for.

Sunny Personality?

January 28, 2023

Today, I just need to be outside the house.

I've got to get new running shoes, so I use that as an excuse to take a couple of hours to myself.

I overshoot. It's a Sunday, and I'm at the shoe store a good hour-and-a-half before it opens.

I decide to walk around Summit, NJ listening to a new playlist I created named "Outlook."

Here are some of the songs on it:

- "What a Wonderful World" - Louis Armstrong (currently my favorite)

- "Somewhere Over the Rainbow" - Israel Kamakawiwo'ole

- "Here Comes the Sun" - The Beatles

As I walk through the neighborhood, I can't help but sing along. I round a corner and I'm singing at the top of my lungs. I glance at a house, and an older woman chuckles to herself.

I smile and wish her a great day and continue singing. It feels kind of nice.

Eventually, I make it to the shoe store and find a pair that I like. When I check out, the cashier says to me, "What a first customer, you're just a sunny person." I smile, and as I leave I'm shocked.

I've never been described as a "sunny" person. It's amazing.

Dense Forest

February 1, 2023

My wife and I are struggling in a dense forest. We're clawing. We're scratching. We're doing everything we can to get out. We see glimpses of light, but it dissipates quickly.

We turn and look at each other. We realize we have to go our separate ways.

She has her way out of the forest. I have mine.

We look around.

We make eye contact one last time.

We nod.

We turn in our directions.

We head off.

As I take my first step, I turn and I see her step. I don't know if she looks at me.

I walk. She walks.

I turn back again, and I see her further away.

I walk. She walks.

Eventually, I look in her direction and I don't see her.

I sit down.

I pull my knees to my chest.

I put my head down.

I cry.

I don't know how long the tears fall, but as they slow, a feeling of hope flows throughout me. I know we have both truly started our journey to happiness.

I look directly behind me where my 42 years of pain follows.

I recognize that it's there, but I also know that from here on out, it will never lead my life again. My life is too short to let the pain lead.

The further I walk, the further it falls. I know that my pain will continue to test me. But I also know I'll get through it.

I know there is a clearing ahead.

I trust that The Universe is guiding me there.

I say to myself: "Just. One. Step. At. A. Time."

One step makes it easy. I can always take one step.

I breathe in.

I breathe out.

I take one last look in her direction.

I send her my love.

I face my own direction.

I take my next step.

Nightly Struggle

February 2, 2023

How do I do this? When I'm alone with my thoughts, all I want to do is sink. I've only ever gotten through it with distraction, but distraction doesn't work anymore.

I can't be on social media. I don't know why.

I wake up at 4 a.m. I can't settle my mind and go back to sleep. Those damn cars outside are too loud. The chirping birds won't let me sleep.

I can't go downstairs or I'll wake the dogs. The dogs will wake the whole house.

I don't want to watch TV. Or rather, I turn it on, and the voices are still there. This dark hole is there. No matter what I do, it's there.

It's always there ... why can't I just be normal?

I lie in bed and my thoughts spiral out of control.

I'm so lost.

Looking Inward

February 3, 2023

I don't get to work from home frequently, but today I do. At lunch, when work starts to slow, it's just me. I get scared when it's just me.

I listen to myself when it's just me.

I sit at the kitchen island to eat. It's my favorite place in the house because I can look out into the sun during this time of day.

The voices are so loud today. Ho'oponopono isn't working. I try to get on my old distraction mechanism of social media, and it doesn't help. In fact, it makes it worse.

I'm at a loss.

Am I getting any better? I thought I was, and yet here I am eating lunch in my favorite spot in a silent house, and it's so deafening.

I turn to the left, and there are these three plaques that have literally hung in my house since we moved in.

"Go confidently in the direction of your dreams."[1]

"Wisdom begins in wonder."[2]

"Who looks outside dreams, who looks inside awakens."[3]

I read the last one and immediately start to cry. I *am* on the right path, I just need to keep working. I've seen these quotes everyday for years and I finally understand what they truly mean.

I'm not supposed to find a place that brings me peace. I'm supposed to find peace in any place.

2nd Support Group Member

February 5, 2023

I'm supposed to be working on these letters from the better parent to my 8-year-old self. I don't know why I picture an 8-year-old me; maybe it's because I saw a goofy picture of myself in the second grade and it made me smile.

I can't decide which parent, and I don't know how to write it.

I post a message in the chat, and someone from California reaches out with how he wrote his letters. Just like the other calls, I start my story with tears. Just like the other calls, he says, "It's okay. I understand. I've been there."

Another person.

"I don't pick the better parent," he says. "I pick the parent responsible. I go through it, I recount the incident, then I continue the letter with an explanation of why they had to do it. Finally, I have the parent tell me what they wish they had done. But I write it like it actually happened. I know it didn't happen that way, but it gives me comfort knowing that they would have if they could have."

That night I start my letters. These letters begin my path of curing the source, not the symptom.

I write more than 30 letters over the next two days, crying as I write every single word.

Dad Letter

February 5, 2023

I've decided not to share the first two parts of the letters. The parts that recount what happened and why it happened. I'll keep that for me, but below is the last part of my first two letters: one to my dad and one to my mom.

Dear Son,

<Written in the first person of what my dad did>

<Written in the first person of why he did it and an apology>

When I think back, I remember five minutes of sitting with you at breakfast eating buttery toast. I'd ask you about what you were excited for, and before I headed out for the long day, I gave you a hug and I kissed your head. I loved those five minutes.

Love, Dad

The last paragraph didn't actually happen. It's what I wished had happened.

Mom Letter

February 5, 2023

Dear Son,

<Written in the first person of what my mom did>

<Written in the first person of why she did what she did and an apology>

I remember playing board games, cards, and trying to figure out the Nintendo. I remember telling happy stories about my life in Vietnam and recounting the amazing events of my escape to reunite with Dad.

But mostly, I remember us spending so many nights together, smiling, sometimes crying, thankful for Dad, but mostly relishing my time with my son.

Love, Mom

Reconnecting With an Old Friend

Early February 2023

An old friend reaches out. I don't really want to speak about my situation, but for some reason I do want to speak with Chris.

I'm at the Princeton Public Library again. We speak for an hour. Just like most conversations at this point, I cry.

He is supportive without question. Chris is the first person in the world to hear me use the word, "suicide." I don't know why I feel compelled to do so, but I do. So, I do.

Chris says, "I wish I would've checked in on you more."

Without hesitation, I respond, "It wouldn't have mattered. I wasn't telling a single soul about it. I planned on leaving the world without anybody knowing."

I realize at that moment that I have lied to the world for 30 years. I decide from here on out that I will only live in truths for the rest of my life.

No More Lies

Mid-February 2023

One of the hardest things in this process is being truthful with my parents.

I got my driver's license when I was 16. On Sundays, I would drive to church and get the church bulletin. I'd leave and go about my day. When I got home, I had the church bulletin and witnesses that I was there in case my dad asks.

Today, I tell my parents on a phone call. My mom said, "Now I know the type of person you really are."

I respond with, "That's right. I can only be me. You can decide whether you want to love me."

I also tell them that they are not going to see my kids or talk to them again until they stop asking them to go to church.

I support them no matter what, and right now, they don't want to go to church.

"I will not put my kids in a situation to lie to you to make you happy," I tell them.

Living my life in truths is hard, but it's freeing.

To me, it's necessary.

Free Books

February 7, 2023

Today I walk to the Princeton Post Office to send something off. On the way back, there is a person giving away free books. Since I can't watch TV or be on social media anymore, I take him up on it.

They are books by Rich Shapero. According to the person handing out the books, Rich is trying to revolutionize reading. There's an accompanying app with a bunch of interactive content for each book.

I try reading the first book, *Dreams of Delphine*, but it's just not to my taste.[1] There is an insert with a QR code to the app, which I download.

The very first piece of content is an interview with Colin Crist as he recounts losing his twin sister at the age of 7. In the video he talks about how his therapist says: "Feelings, no matter how powerful or painful, are part of us, and our bodies can experience them without damage. It's better to experience them than suppress them as that does cause problems."[2]

I use it as more justification that I'm on the right path. I suppressed feelings for so long and look where it got me.

The tears have been streaming daily. I know that exponentially more are on their way.

Replay a Scene

February 7, 2023

As I start to address the source, I realize that I could start working on my inner voice.

"We are not responsible for what our eyes are seeing. We are responsible for how we perceive what we are seeing," says best-selling author Gabrielle Bernstein.[1]

My mental health professional asks me to remember a time that was particularly hard. The first one that comes to mind is when I was trying to discipline one of my kids and they couldn't stop crying.

"What do you see?" he says.

"I see a dad who doesn't know what to do. He's not doing a good job. He's causing his kiddo, whom he loves, so much pain. He's not the dad they need," I respond.

"Look again," he says.

"What do you mean?" I am puzzled.

"Are you there?" he asks.

I nod.

"Well, that's good," he continues, "Are you hitting them?"

"No, I would never," I respond.

He nods, "Well, that's good too, so look again, what do you see?"

That's when it hits me. If I can't think two things about myself at the exact same moment, and I've cleared the source of my pain, then I get to pick what I tell myself.

Why wouldn't I give myself grace?

3rd Support Group Member

February 8, 2023

"Nothing goes my way," I put into the group chat.

A third member reaches out to me. After swapping stories, I cry again. It's followed immediately by, "It's okay. I understand. I've been there."

Goodness, I can't hear that enough.

"What's going on?" he asks.

"Work, life, everything just doesn't go the way I plan. It's nothing to do with my narrative to myself; everything just goes wrong, and it's adding so much stress," I respond.

"It has everything to do with your narrative to yourself," he says. "Have you worked on the Black Stamp?" he asks.

"No, what's that?"

"It's one of Larry Bilotta's methods. When things go wrong most of the people in the world look at things in two lights."

"Red Stamp: I don't like it; I won't accept it."

"Green Stamp: I don't like it, but I'll accept it."

"You've got to Black Stamp it, or say to yourself, 'I accept it, and this is good.'"

"You can't control anything in this world except for what's in your mind, so don't fight it. Figure out the good from the situation, and then accept it. Sometimes the good is only what you can learn, and that's okay because learning is good."[1]

Music Returns

February 9, 2023

As my head starts to clear and life starts to seem bearable, I rediscover other things I used to love. On this day, I spend the better part of an afternoon—and hours into the night—just plucking on the guitar.

A couple of weeks later, the piano comes back in full force. I hate when someone hears my mistakes. It must be perfect before I can play in front of people.

That's when I realized I have a Golden Book with the piano. Growing up, while practicing piano, my mom would stand ten feet behind me in the kitchen. Every time I messed up, she'd sigh or say they were wasting money on my lessons.

I run my toolkit on it, and the next morning I play for hours. Everybody is home, and I don't care how rusty I sound.

Another breakthrough.

I call this process "Sherlock Mode" or "Sherlocking." When I feel off, I try to figure out the source. I ask myself, "Is my current situation the actual cause of my stress?"

If it is, great! I can process it and let it go. If it's not my current situation, I go into "Sherlock Mode" and find out which event in my past is affecting my present.

Inner Child Visit

February 15, 2023

As I've shared my tools, I've learned so many more from others who have gone through therapy. There's a cascade of tools out there. You need to find the ones that work for you.

Dr. Diana Raab says, "Each one of us has an inner child" [...] "Getting in touch with your inner child can help foster well-being and bring a lightness to life."[1]

I like this tool a lot because in this one, I'm the one providing the comfort.

I visit my past. As 42-year-old me, I sit with little me and validate that inner child.

I saw an 8-year-old me, sitting crisscross with his elbows on his knees and resting his head on his hands, looking down at the ground. He's living right in the middle of a Golden Book. He's hurting. He's so confused. He's so sad all the time.

I walk up to him and mimic how he sits. I look him in the eye. I tell him, "It doesn't matter what goes on out there. I will forever be here with you. I will always choose you. I will love you forever."

Unconditional Love. I start to love myself ... my whole self.

To this day, the first thing I do is visit my 8-year-old self. These days, he's usually in a field hitting a balloon up into the sky. He waits for it to fall and taps it back up. I tell him every day, "It doesn't matter what goes on out in the world, it's the two of us together. Forever."

Shuttlecock & Birdie

Mid-February 2023

I post in the chat, "My two youngest bicker, do you guys have any ideas?"

The chatter starts from multiple guys, and a discussion ensues.

"I bet they don't start off arguing and shouting right away," someone says.

"It builds," suggests another.

"It starts with a look, and then a comment, and it escalates," still another.

That night, I figure out a way to talk with the kids about it. I had just picked up the garage a bit the night before and tried to organize the badminton items.

That's when it hit me.

After dinner that night, as we're doing chores, I ask them if they're open to a new idea. They nod.

"Okay, I know you both love each other. Every time I'm one-on-one with you, you think of kind things you want to do for each other; it's not until you're together that things escalate." I continue, "When you are mean to each other, it's a different you. It's the mean voice on your shoulder. Let's call him Voldemort."

"I like Voldemort; maybe Umbridge for me," the younger one says.

I laugh a little, and nod.

"Okay, Voldemort and Umbridge play badminton. Each can only play if the other hits the shuttlecock back. If you decide to take control of Voldemort, then Umbridge doesn't have any more fun trying to hit a shuttlecock, because the shuttlecock isn't returned.

"Each time you let Voldemort or Umbridge hit the shuttlecock, it escalates. But you guys love each other. I see that all the time when you're not together. So let's work on dropping the shuttlecock. You both have a chance to drop it. You game?" I ask.

They both nod.

"Cool. I'll start off by reminding you when I see a shuttlecock, but at some point, it'll become a habit and you'll find it on your own," I say.

The next Monday, I celebrate their achievement of a zero-shuttlecock night.

I think to myself, "If it works with negative stuff, I bet it does with the positive stuff too."

They share multiple chores in the house. Folding clothes and setting the table are two of them. Two nights later, the younger, recognizing that the older had to stay late for school, decided to fold all the clothes and put them away.

When it comes time to set the table, the older one says, "You know what? You folded all the clothes, so I'll set the whole table."

I tear up, and I stop everybody. They think something's wrong. I say, "Let's call this a birdie," adding, "Things don't just escalate on the negative side. They do on the positive side too. When each of you does something kind, the other reciprocates."

We live in a world full of stresses, so shuttlecocks still get hit; but there's no doubt in my mind that they have a tool that they can use all their lives.

When it gets too intense, I step in and take the shuttlecock away.

Otherwise, I try to lead by example, hitting as many birdies as I can.

I hit birdies to strangers with a smile. Most of the time, they smile back. It's always nice to get a smile.

Sometimes, I get a weird look, a shuttlecock. I drop it because I don't know what their day has been like. Maybe they're where I was in early January. I give them some grace.

My Paradise

February 19, 2023

The water transforms.

The tidal wave is now a flowing stream.

Grass is growing. Flowers are blooming. The bugs and bees squirm about.

The trees shoot up. The majestic birds fly overhead. Other animals come. Bunnies, deer, moose, squirrels, and chipmunks roam as I sit on my little park bench playing music and writing in my journal.

I realize that the clearing I was walking towards was one that I was creating.

When I piece that together, I write it down in my journal in all caps.

Validation & Support

February 22, 2023

Today an old colleague texts me. He made a mistake at work and was worried that he would lose his job over it. I look at my schedule and set a time to call him later in the day.

I listen to him speak for over an hour as he explains the entire situation; how his mistake cost the company hundreds of thousands of dollars; how he was sure he was going to lose his job over it.

When he finishes, I say, "I can see why you feel that way. It totally sucks."

He believes what he feels. So first, I validate his feelings, just like all of the guys did when I told them my story.

Then I go through and ask him to look at the worst possible scenario. I learned this from one of the guys in the group who is a Professor Adam Grant fan. Before Grant has a stressful presentation, he goes through the worst-case scenario. At the end of that walkthrough, he acknowledges that he's still okay, and then he can put it aside and let the stress go. He doesn't live in the worst-case scenario; he just acknowledges that it's possible and goes on from there.[1]

I walk him through it.

"If you lose your job, what's the worst that can happen?" I ask.

He goes through the scenario.[2]

When he finishes, I say, "That doesn't sound too bad, right? And you'll get a lot of golf time in the spring."

He calms down.

Then I ask him, "Has anybody in the company said anything about you losing your job? You've done so much for them over the past three years."

"No," he says.

"Well, if no one has said anything about that, then why choose to live there? All it's doing is causing you stress. Furthermore, now you know that if the worst-case scenario happens, you'll be okay."

Good Enough

March 1, 2023

On this day, we switch my sessions from focusing on forgiveness to believing that I am good enough for this world. I did a Psych-K session with Stephanie focusing on the following:[1]

Therapy Notes:

- Today, I now know that I am good enough.

- I take responsibility for my own happiness.

- I am *valuable* and I *matter*.

Reunion: Scene 1

March 2, 2023

Tonight, a scene comes to my head. It's the last night that my dad was in Vietnam before leaving for what he thought was less than two years but turned into five years.

This scene doesn't actually happen in real life. Nobody remembers what happened on that last night.

I'm not a screenwriter, but I pull out my laptop and transcribe.

Ten minutes later, I'm heaving and sobbing, and on my laptop screen sit four pages.

Scene 1.

Reunion: It's A Movie

March 3, 2023

I send the scene to Chris, my close friend who I first told about my suicidal past.

"SEND MORE PAGES!!" is his text response.

"Damn," I think to myself, "It's a movie."

I realize he's going to write the musical score. Chris has played piano for decades and wrote a musical in college.

I ask him. He joins.

We start our last careers.

Reunion: Completed Outline

March 10, 2023

Over the next week, scenes flow into my mind. They come from all different directions and are dispersed throughout the movie. All I can do in my free time is write and outline.

This morning, I tell Chris that during my kids' spring break, we'll have to work on this stuff together in-person. He asks if I think I could get it done.

I tell him, probably the outline.

That very afternoon, I finish the entire out-line at Elitist Coffee in South Orange, NJ. When I outline the last two scenes, I openly bawl.

I take a few seconds to force breaths, wipe away tears with both hands, and then franti-cally go back to typing. I'm sure the people there think I'm weird, but I don't care.

Dinner with a Friend

March 13, 2023

Tonight, I have dinner with a friend from college. I share with a second person that suicide was only a matter of time. Our dinner, intended to be an hour, goes on for three. I don't eat much. I tell him everything, and we both cry at different times.

I consider him one of my closest friends, and tonight was the first time I really let myself connect with him.

He reminds me that in college I used to walk around telling people I'd die early. I was the only 21-year-old saying that.

As I write this now, I realize I did die early, because that version of me no longer exists.

Like my first and favorite tattoo, the phoenix, I've burned up and have been re-born.

Reunion: Draft 1

March 16, 2023

At 11:58 p.m. tonight, exactly 14 days after Scene 1, I finish my first draft of *Reunion*. It's interesting that I finish on the 16th, as my parents real-life reunion also happened on a 16th.

I could label this section Therapy Notes too, because every single impactful scene came with an uncountable number of tears.

I fall asleep with a million emotions: happiness, sadness, accomplishment, joy, understanding, gratitude, and ultimately, unbounded love.

For a brief second, I think, *if only I had figured this out earlier*. I'd have a movie, not a screenplay. But I quickly conclude that this had to happen the way it did.

I now have a different relationship with my past. Today, I look back on regret and think of this quote from Syanna Wand: "I wish I would have done that differently, and, at that time, I couldn't."[1]

I give my past self grace—because that past self is me.

Reunion: The Next Two Weeks

I read the script to anybody who wants to listen. I send it everywhere. I notice that those who preface reading or listening with, "I don't know if I'll give any good feedback," give the best notes.

I am lucky enough to find a couple of working screenwriters who are blunt with me.

I work.

By the time I leave for spring break, I have a fifth draft. I print out seven copies—a first print for any of my screenplays.

By the time I submit it to a screenplay writing competition in June, I've already sent it to everybody in my little bubble and to over 28 "strangers." I quote "strangers" because I believe that we're all connected, so they're not really strangers.

If they want to read it, great! If not, no worries. I've had fun speaking with them a bit and sharing my dream of making a movie.

My Work Team

March 21, 2023

I realize that I need to share my story with my team at work—a team that knew something was wrong, but didn't know what.

So I share. I cry in front of them. Some of them cry with me. I tell them about the life insurance, I tell them about the therapy, I tell them it was only a matter of time.

Then I tell them that I am proud of them, because as I took my mental space, they flourished.

When I started therapy, my philosophy to leading a team changed. I shift my focus away from the tasks assigned to them. I refocus on them. I focus on their approach to problems. I focus on making sure they had space between their working lives and personal lives. I focus on making things easier for them.

I help with the car, but I let them drive.

I've had the title of "leader" for so long, but it's the first time I feel like a true leader.

My Time

April 5, 2023

It's the middle of spring break. I am "playing," as my sister likes to refer to it now. Writing the screenplays, working on the music with Chris, writing lyrics, giving feedback on melodies. It does feel more like playing than working.

We're having a blast playing with *Reunion* and reviewing the half-written second screenplay I've also started, an original called *Love*.

At about 10 p.m., I call it a night. Some of the kids wonder why I go to bed so early.

"It's because I automatically wake up at 4 a.m.," I reply.

There is a difference now. I go to bed early to preserve my ability to wake up at 4 a.m. I love those early morning hours when it's just me and my thoughts.

The world is quiet, and I can sit in the calm. I'll usually meditate for half an hour, and then I follow where my intuition leads me for the next couple of hours.

Most days, I write. Other days, I listen to music. Still others, I lie quietly in bed and listen to the silence. The silence then turns into birds chirping and the sound of cars driving by as people start their day. I wonder what their story is. I hope it's a good one. Then I wish them a wonderful day. "Wonderful" is my new favorite word, by the way.

There's only one constant in the early morning hours, it's just me, and it's: wonderful.

That's Enough

April 7, 2023

Today is the first time I'm seeing my parents in person since Christmas.

My dad has recently gotten into the habit of texting me and telling me to call my mom to cheer her up.

"You're causing her so much pain," he says. "Call her every day so she knows you're okay."

Up until today, I called as much as I could. I feel bad, and I call to listen to her say, "Do you understand that you turning away from God is causing me so much pain? You need to come back to the Church."

I tell them that I'm not responsible for their happiness. "I've said it so many times. I am happier now than I've ever been. It's up to you to decide whether or not you believe me. I can't keep trying to convince you, so I won't," I respond to my mom.

I turn to my dad and say, "Please do not text me to call mom anymore. I love you both more today than I ever have before. I know what struggles you've been through. But it's not my job to make you happy. That's your job. Only you can do that for yourselves. You can't even do it for each other."

They hear the words, but I'm not sure they listen to them. All I can do is be me; they will choose whether they want to love me.

What I Needed

April 13, 2023

I call one of the support group guys. I talk to all of them regularly. We chat for a while, and then he says something interesting: "My relationships were need-based."

I did the same thing. It was *my* need. I *needed* to be involved in everything. I *needed* people to like me in order to be okay.

But when I hit rock-bottom, I realized that what I really needed was to heal.

When I finally decided to heal, everything opened up for me. When I was open and clear, my relationships with everyone around me opened up.

My team performs better. They know I have their back. My children and I have the best relationships we've ever had. I actually connect with my friends, it's not superficial.

As for me, what do I need now? Nothing really. If it weren't for real-world responsibilities, I would be completely at peace with access to a piano, my guitar, and my journal.

My Last Session

April 13, 2023

Yesterday was my last Psych-K session.

As we finish, we get personal for a bit.

"I don't think there are any coincidences," she says, "I believe everything happens for a reason. I think we all choose our parents, and I think you chose yours."

As I reflect, I think she's right. I've always wanted to do good in this world, so The Universe let me pick my parents. It knew that I'd be brave enough to share my story, but for me to use that bravery to help the most people, I had to live through that pain. I had to get to a place dark enough to take my own life for so many years.

The Universe also put the right people in my life at the right time to keep me here until the time was right.

My ex-wife once said to me, "Trauma moves through families until someone is willing to feel it."

Boy, did I feel it. All of it.

The Universe has love for all of us, and all we can do is trust.

Reunion: Substantial Completion

April 13, 2023

I stole "substantial completion" from the energy industry. It signifies that the majority of the work is done, but it's not finished.

I feel like today I've substantially completed *Reunion*.

Over the past couple of months, I've gotten to know the staff at the Princeton Public Library. The woman who runs the coffee shop is retiring. She asks me, "What do you do?"

My response anytime that question comes up is, "Well, by day I run IT for a start-up, and at night I write screenplays." I usually let the person decide where to take the conversation from there, because I can talk endlessly about both.

She picks the screenplay route, and I tell her about *Reunion*. I ask her if she'll read it and give me feedback.

I'm convinced if you've seen any movie, you can at least tell me if you'd watch this one.

"I don't read, and I don't think I can give any good feedback" she says, "but I'll give it a shot."

I know her feedback will be incredible. My best notes have come from people who say something like that.

Two days later—her last day working at the coffee shop, she says, "I couldn't put it down."

"Oh!! Yay!! Okay, feedback please! Honest feedback. You won't hurt my feelings," I plead.

"First, I would definitely watch it. I am also so glad you made it a happy ending. I was worried there at the end, and I was going to hurt you if you didn't. I just wish I knew what happened to them."

A lightbulb comes on in my head. I immediately sit down and write in a photo section right before the end credits. I figure out how to get a baby picture of *me* into the movie too.

I come back up to the register, open my laptop, and I read her the new sequence. I start to cry. I always know I'm onto something if I cry.

"Hahaha, I got you going, didn't I?" she laughs.

I smile and nod, "It's exactly what the movie needed, and it gives closure to the audience. When you and your family go and watch the movie, you'll get to tell your family that your feedback inspired this final sequence."

She laughs and says, "Oh, I can't wait! I'm staying until the end!"

I don't know if I'll ever see her again, but she seems like she has a happy life. I'm glad to have met her.

I thank her for the small interactions we had over the past few months, give her a hug, and wish her the most wonderful retirement.

Enjoy the Ride

April 14, 2023

This morning I speak to one of the guys, and he says, "Don't forget to enjoy the process. Enjoy the ride. You're on a pretty good one."

Throughout these three months, different guys in the group have been repeating, "Enjoy it." Early in January, I had thought to myself, "How in the world can I enjoy this?"

Today I recognize that pulling myself out of the dark place is the ride. Pulling myself out with the help of so many, and connecting to so many, is the ride. Slowly finding the beauty in every little thing in this world is the ride.

Every second of every hour of every day, I made progress. I still make progress.

And when a challenge presents itself, I learn.

They're all so right.

"Enjoy it" … and boy did I.

I still do.

I'll Listen

April 14, 2023

Since I've started sharing my story, people share with me. Someone's brother tried to commit suicide; another's sister; another's son. These are people that I interact with all the time, and I never knew.

A woman tells me that she sees countless similarities to my story, but that she isn't as deep in the dark as I was. She cries while telling me. I cry with her.

Someone else recently shared that his son is dying. That one hit me the hardest. I can't even come close to imagining his pain.

I let everyone talk for as long or as little as they want. I validate them and offer my support.

I think that's why this is so important to me. Every single person in this world goes through pain, and for some reason our society teaches us to keep it bottled up. *"Keep the emotions inside, emotions are weak."*

That's what I did for so long with my brick wall. But as we talk about them, we can feel them. When we feel them, we can process them. And when we process them, we *all* become stronger.

John Purkiss:
I Am

April 17, 2023

I haven't been actively looking for any new books to read at this point, but something about the blue butterfly on the cover of *The Power of Letting Go* catches my eye.[1] A friend once told me, "Books come to us when we're ready. They're magical like that."

I read the entire book in a single day. It's uncanny how much John Purkiss' tools resemble my own; so much so that I wonder if he worked with my mental health professional. Alas, he did not.

There are two tools I immediately start using myself.

One of the concepts he talks about is being 'here now.'[2]—something that I now aim for. But every so often, that chatter starts up. Not the suicide voices—those are gone—but the other voices.

What will happen tomorrow? What does this other person think of me? Why did I screw that up yesterday? What if I'm late for work? Did I say something wrong? What do they think I said? Remember to pay this bill. Don't forget to wake up the kids for school. Put away the dishes. Vacuum. Fold the clothes. Feed the dogs.

On and on and on and on and on.

He suggests what I consider to be a halfway meditation.[3] You can do it anywhere; you can do it right in the middle of a conversation if you need to. The voices speak in the middle of a conversation, so why not do this in the middle of a conversation?

Focus your attention on two words: "I Am ."[4]

Purkiss continues, "Keep thinking it over and over like a mantra ... You aren't identifying with anything. You simply are."[5]

When I use this second tool, I find myself calming down, and I mentally take a step away from the voices to be myself. I know that everything will get done, and if they don't all get done right away, it's not a big deal.

Maybe I will need to make a second trip to Target. Is that really such a problem? Heck, what if I meet a producer in the checkout line? Who knows?

I literally use this tool multiple times a day.

Keep Working

April 18, 2023

A couple of days ago, I did something that hurt someone I care for. It was completely unintentional. I got overzealous in my desire to do good and forgot to consider their feelings.

I apologize to them, but unlike other things lately, it sticks with me. I can't figure out what was going on.

I initiate my "Sherlock Mode." As I go through the process, I realize that I still wasn't forgiving myself. It wasn't something from my childhood, but nevertheless, I was holding on to it because of how much I cared for the person. I wasn't processing or resolving it.

Feel the feelings, and then follow where they go. They'll tell you what you need to work on.

This time, I combine my past tools with a new one from John Purkiss. I 'relive the experience and resolve the issue.'[1] In addition, I revisit myself from a couple of days ago, and I forgive him.

He and I are the same.

"You did what you thought was right. What's done is done. Learn from it, let it go, and make sure you consider their feelings in the future."

Once I do those two processes together, I feel a sense of relief and calmness.

It reinforces the fact that I must always keep learning, and I continually need to give myself grace.

I've committed to doing that for the rest of my life.

Time

April 26, 2023

Today I receive some news that reminds me how short life can be. That's a story for another time. No matter how many years you are given in this world, they're never enough.

I know that now.

I call my mom. She immediately talks about church again, and I remind her that I don't want to talk about religion anymore.

This time, she stops. She doesn't argue, and she moves on. We speak for an uncomfortable minute or so.

At the end of the conversation, I finish with, "I love you."

"Thank you," she responds.

It's not exactly what I want to hear, but it's definitely better than other things she's said to me.

There's hope there. Hope that she'll eventually tell me she loves me. The real me.

Only time will tell.

All I can do is surrender and trust The Universe.

43

May 1, 2023

Today is my 43rd birthday. Is it what I expected it to be? No, there are a lot of things that are different today than when I turned 42. But you know what? The weekend celebrations were so much fun. I spent time with college friends, including one that surprised me by flying in just to have dinner Saturday night. Sunday, the kids and I went to Disney100: The Exhibition in Philadelphia, and then we eat at Sugar Factory.

Today, I take a half-day off work and play both the guitar and piano. I finish my night with writing.

When I reflect on 42, I know it could've gone in so many different directions. Every possibility was just as real as this one.

My life could've been cut short in January. Instead, I fell in love with myself.

It's interesting that what my mom said to me has helped me get to here—those words she spoke to me in the middle of January, "Stop crying and be a man." Six total words that led me to the fact that I wasn't innately messed up.

Five one-syllable words added to the word "crying."

The two-syllable word is the lasting one.

I spoke to Chris the other day and he said, "Crying isn't just associated with sadness. We cry with all emotions if we let it."

I don't hold the tears back anymore.

Life still gets hard. There are logistics; there are work stresses; there are a million different things to deal with. I can't just go into the mountains and live with my music and writing. But when I think about it, I don't want to run away. I want to live this life.

A co-worker said to me last Wednesday, "Life has troughs and peaks," but I know my troughs will never get to where they were in January. Now I have my toolkit, and I choose to use it.

When the tools don't work, I seek more. The work never stops. I choose this new life every day.

One of my favorite quotes that has continually come up in my life over and over again is from *The Hitchhiker's Guide to the Galaxy*: "The Answer to the Great Question" [...] "Of Life, the Universe, and Everything" [...] "Is" [...] "Forty-two."[1]

I don't think it's a coincidence that I learned how to truly be happy at 42.

It's Love. The answer is *Love*.

It's simple; it's all there. I needed to unconditionally love myself.

After I do that, I turn that unconditional love outward. I unconditionally love everyone and everything that comes into my life. Doing that makes life *incredible*. It makes life *amazing*. It makes life *worth living*. It makes life full of *awe*.

It makes life *wonderful*.

Her Way

May 17, 2023

I follow my intuition every day, and I hear it say, "Call Mom." I do. The conversations are short. They're not deep or insightful, but they're nice, and they cheer her up a bit.

I don't know why my inner voice keeps saying to call her. Then it hits me: Recently, I've come to unconditionally love everyone and everything. The world is beautiful when I do.

The Universe was telling me to show my mom—the single person who's caused the most pain in my life. She and I will likely never have a deep emotional connection the same way I do with others, but that's okay. She's had too much pain in her life to open up like that.

This morning, she tells me about flowers that she used to plant. Days later, a family friend brings us a small bouquet of yellow flowers. I put them in a vase by the sink.

My first chore of the day is emptying the dishwasher, and my last chore of the day is washing the dishes. I see the flowers each time and it reminds me a bit of her. It reminds me that no matter how hard life is, I can always find the beauty in it.

The Universe was telling me to accept her ... to love her and our relationship for what it is. She was the last person I really needed to open myself up to.

I keep calling her. I end every call with, "I love you." She ends every call with, "Thank you."

Maybe that's just her way.

The Beach

May 27, 2023

It's Memorial Day weekend. I take my kids to Wildwood, NJ, for a couple of days. Today we spend the entire day on the beach.

I watch my son sitting in a chair, his feet buried in the sand, as he listens to a funny video in one ear and the sound of the ocean in the other.

I watch my 13-year-old lying on a beach towel, talking on the phone to her older sister. She ends the call with, "I love you." She gets up and walks to my 11-year-old to help her build a volcano in the sand.

I watch families sit together. Some people are on phones, some are reading, some sit with their eyes closed.

I watch groups of friends, or maybe groups of strangers, playing beach sports. I watch people flying kites. I watch people searching for shells. I watch a couple walking on the beach holding hands.

They smile with every action.

It's beautiful. My life is beautiful. Their lives are beautiful. All of our lives are beautiful.

So let's live them. Let's feel them.

I remember Chris say, "[Crying] isn't just associated with sadness." So ...

I sit with my legs pulled to my chest.

I keep my head up.

I feel the beauty unfold around me.

I cry.

How I Live Now

At this very moment, I sit outside on Princeton's campus. When I look up, I see a flowering tree.

I spent three months of my life growing into a man on this campus. A man that is stronger because he is emotionally vulnerable.

I live my life very differently now. I have three simple daily goals:

1. Good: Find the good and the beauty in every little thing

2. Gratitude: Express gratitude every chance I get

3. Love: Unconditionally love *myself* and *everyone*

When I'm able to do those things, my day is easy. If I can't, it's no big deal. In those final seconds before I fall asleep, I tell myself, "You did the best you could and tomorrow is a new day."

Meanwhile, *today*. Today, I'll tell my story. And when I'm done, if you want me to listen to yours, I'll listen.

I'll listen. I'll cry with you, and when you're done telling me your story, I'll say, "It's okay. I understand. I've been there."

Then I'll add, "And just like me, I know *you* belong."

About the Author

I'm a simple storyteller based in Maplewood, NJ. I spent the first twenty years of my professional career in tech. After finally facing my suicidal past with 400 hours of therapy in 10 weeks, writing spilled out.

Notes

Golden Books

1. Little Golden Books. New York, New York: Penguin Random House, n.d.

Ho'oponopono

1. "Exploring Ho'oponopono: The Hawaiian Art of Forgiveness and Healing." centreofexcellence.com. Centre of Excellence, accessed 8/10/24, https://www.centreofexcellence. com/what-is-hooponopono/.

2. Yeo, Diane. "Mindful Monday: A Simple Prayer." Diane Yeo Mindfulness. July 17,

2023. https://www.dianeyeo.com/blog/
2023/7/17/mindful-monday-a-simple-pray
er .

3. "Exploring Ho'oponopono."

Looking Inward

1. "Go confidently in the direction of
your dreams. Live the life you have
imagined." buboquote.com. buboquote,
accessed 8/10/24, https://www.bubo
quote.com/en/quote/4267-thoreau-go-
confidently-in-the-direction-of-your-dreams-
live-the-life-you-have-imagined.

2. Peeples, Shanna. *Think Like Socrates:
Using Questions to Invite Wonder & Em-
pathy Into theClassroom*. Thousand Oaks,
California: Corwin, 2019.

3. Venstra, Elizabeth. *True Genius: 1001 Quotes That Will Change Your Life*. New York City, New York: Skyhorse Publishing, 2008.

Free Books

1. Shapero, Rich. *Dreams of Delphine*. Rich Shapero, 2022.

2. Crist, Colin. "Rich Shapero - Dreams of Delphine - Chapter 1 'Losing My Tw in.'" Interview by Rich Shapero and Too-Far Media, July 18, 2022. YouTubeVideo, 4:32. https://youtu.be/l8A-NBr_pEY?si=4 T6x-3hdniuWO6wT.

Replay a Scene

1. Bernstein, Gabrielle. *The Universe Has Your Back: Transform Fear to Faith*. Carlsbad, California: Hay House Publishing, 2018.

3rd Support Group Member

1. Bilotta, Larry. "3 Mistakes To Avoid When Your Spouse Says It's Over," larrybilotta.com. Life Discoveries Inc., accessed August 10, 2024. https://larrybilotta.com/.

Inner Child Visit

1. Healthline. "Finding and Getting to Know Your Inner Child," June 26, 2020. https://www.healthline.com/health/inner-child.

Validation & Support

1. Grant, Adam. "Organizational psychologist and bestselling author," adamgrant.net. Accessed August 10, 2024. https://adamgrant.net.

2. Grant, Adam. "Organizational psychologist and bestselling author."

Good Enough

1. "Psych-k, Rejuv-u, Subconscious, Conscious, Hypnosis, Quantum Energy." Psych-k. 2013. https://rejuv-u.com/index.html.

Reunion: Draft 1

1. Ward, Syanna. 2022. "Bothcan be true. Both probably ARE true." Instagram, December 20, 2022. https://www.instagram.com/syannawand/p/CmZmdtquYTc/.

John Purkiss: I Am

1. Purkiss, John. *The Power of Letting Go: How to drop everything that's holding you back.* London, England: Aster Publishing LTD, 2020.

2. Purkiss, John. *The Power of Letting Go.*
3. Purkiss, John. *The Power of Letting Go.*
4. Purkiss, John. *The Power of Letting Go.*
5. Purkiss, John. *The Power of Letting Go.*

ANHTUẤN ĐỖ

Keep Working
1.Purkiss, John. *The Power of Letting Go.*

43
1. Adams, Douglas. *The Hitchhiker's Guide to the Galaxy: The Illustrated Edition.* Del Rey, 2007.

120

A Space for You

Made in the USA
Middletown, DE
18 October 2024

62866544R00076